CAMBRIDGE LIBRARY COLLECTION

Books of enduring scholarly value

Fiction and Poetry

Reading became an increasingly popular entertainment in eighteenth- and nineteenth-century Britain, Europe and America, reaching an ever wider spectrum of society as the cost of printing came down and levels of literacy rose. The novels avidly consumed in this period were not merely escapist fiction. Many of them drew attention to serious social issues such as slavery, child labour and other forms of exploitation that blighted the age of revolutions and empire, some were thinly disguised autobiographies, while others had clear educational aims: thus the line between fiction and non-fiction was a fluid one. Poetry too flourished across a wide range of genres, and the political and social agendas of the Romantic movement in particular led to its being read and appreciated at all levels of society. In this series, the Cambridge Library Collection offers the texts of fiction and poetry as these works were first published and received by an eager reading public.

Casa Guidi Windows

In 1847, Elizabeth Barrett Browning (1806–61) moved with her new husband to an apartment in Florence, in the wake of perhaps the most famous literary courtship of the nineteenth century. She soon took to calling their home the Casa Guidi. From there, she observed the events of the early Risorgimento. It was at this time that she produced some of her finest work, including *Aurora Leigh* and *Casa Guidi Windows*. An impressionistic and thoroughly atypical landmark in the Romantic canon, the latter was written in two parts, separated by several years. Beginning with the memory of a singing child and a lush description of Florence's beauty, the first part explores the air of optimism that permeates both the city and the narrator. By the second, disillusionment is rife: Florence has become the scene of demonstrations and broken political promises. This reissue of the 1851 first edition includes Barrett Browning's own introduction.

Cambridge University Press has long been a pioneer in the reissuing of out-of-print titles from its own backlist, producing digital reprints of books that are still sought after by scholars and students but could not be reprinted economically using traditional technology. The Cambridge Library Collection extends this activity to a wider range of books which are still of importance to researchers and professionals, either for the source material they contain, or as landmarks in the history of their academic discipline.

Drawing from the world-renowned collections in the Cambridge University Library and other partner libraries, and guided by the advice of experts in each subject area, Cambridge University Press is using state-of-the-art scanning machines in its own Printing House to capture the content of each book selected for inclusion. The files are processed to give a consistently clear, crisp image, and the books finished to the high quality standard for which the Press is recognised around the world. The latest print-on-demand technology ensures that the books will remain available indefinitely, and that orders for single or multiple copies can quickly be supplied.

The Cambridge Library Collection brings back to life books of enduring scholarly value (including out-of-copyright works originally issued by other publishers) across a wide range of disciplines in the humanities and social sciences and in science and technology.

Casa Guidi Windows

Elizabeth Barrett Browning

CAMBRIDGE UNIVERSITY PRESS

Cambridge, New York, Melbourne, Madrid, Cape Town,
Singapore, São Paolo, Delhi, Mexico City

Published in the United States of America by Cambridge University Press, New York

www.cambridge.org
Information on this title: www.cambridge.org/9781108059916

This edition first published 1851
This digitally printed version 2013

ISBN 978-1-108-06038-7 Hardback
ISBN 978-1-108-05991-6 Paperback

CASA GUIDI WINDOWS.

A Poem.

BY

ELIZABETH BARRETT BROWNING.

LONDON:
CHAPMAN & HALL, 193, PICCADILLY.
1851.

ADVERTISEMENT.

THIS Poem contains the impressions of the writer upon events in Tuscany of which she was a witness. "From a window," the critic may demur. She bows to the objection in the very title of her work. No continuous narrative, nor exposition of political philosophy, is attempted by her. It is a simple story of personal impressions, whose only value is in the intensity with which they were received, as proving her warm affection for a beautiful and unfortunate country; and the sincerity with which they are related, as indicating her own good faith and freedom from all partisanship.

Of the two parts of this Poem, the first was written nearly three years ago, while the second resumes the actual situation of 1851. The discrepancy between the two parts is a sufficient guarantee to the public of the truthfulness of the writer, who, though she certainly escaped the epidemic "falling sickness" of enthusiasm for Pio Nono, takes shame upon herself that she believed, like a woman, some royal oaths, and lost sight of the probable consequences of some obvious popular defects. If the discrepancy should be painful to the reader, let him understand that to the writer it has been more so. But such discrepancy we are called upon to accept at every hour by the conditions of our nature . . . the discrepancy between aspiration and performance, between faith and dis-illusion, between hope and fact.

> "O trusted, broken prophecy,
> O richest fortune sourly crost,
> Born for the future, to the future lost!"

Nay, not lost to the future in this case. The future of Italy shall not be disinherited.

FLORENCE, 1851.

CASA GUIDI WINDOWS.

PART I.

I.

I HEARD last night a little child go singing
'Neath Casa Guidi windows, by the church,
"*O bella libertà, O bella!*" stringing
The same words still on notes he went in search
So high for, you concluded the upspringing
Of such a nimble bird to sky from perch
Must leave the whole bush in a tremble green;
And that the heart of Italy must beat,

While such a voice had leave to rise serene
'Twixt church and palace of a Florence street!—
A little child, too, who not long had been
By mother's finger steadied on his feet;
And still *O bella libertà* he sang.

II.

Then I thought, musing, of the innumerous
Sweet songs which for this Italy outrang
From older singers' lips, who sang not thus
Exultingly and purely, yet, with pang
Sheathed into music, touched the heart of us
So finely that the pity scarcely pained!
I thought how Filicaja led on others,
Bewailers for their Italy enchained,
And how they called her childless among mothers,

Widow of empires, ay, and scarce refrained
Cursing her beauty to her face, as brothers
Might a shamed sister,—"Had she been less fair
She were less wretched,"—how, evoking so
From congregated wrong and heaped despair
Of men and women writhing under blow,
Harrowed and hideous in their filthy lair,
A personating Image, wherein woe
Was wrapt in beauty from offending much,
They called it Cybele, or Niobe,
Or laid it corpse-like on a bier for such,
Where the whole world might drop for Italy
Those cadenced tears which burn not where they touch,—
"Juliet of nations, canst thou die as we?
And was the violet crown that crowned thy head

So over large, though new buds made it rough,
It slipped down and across thine eyelids dead,
O sweet, fair Juliet?"—Of such songs enough;
Too many of such complaints! Behold, instead,
Void at Verona, Juliet's marble trough!
And void as that is, are all images
Men set between themselves and actual wrong,
To catch the weight of pity, meet the stress
Of conscience; though 'tis easier to gaze long
On personations, masks, and effigies,
Than to see live weak creatures crushed by strong.

III.

For me who stand in Italy to-day,
Where worthier poets stood and sang before,
I kiss their footsteps, yet their words gainsay:

I can but muse in hope upon this shore
  Of golden Arno, as it shoots away
Straight through the heart of Florence, 'neath the four
  Bent bridges, seeming to strain off like bows,
And tremble, while the arrowy undertide
  Shoots on and cleaves the marble as it goes,
And strikes up palace-walls on either side,
  And froths the cornice out in glittering rows,
With doors and windows quaintly multiplied,
  And terrace-sweeps, and gazers upon all,
By whom if flower or kerchief were thrown out,
  From any lattice there, the same would fall
Into the river underneath, no doubt,—
  It runs so close and fast 'twixt wall and wall.
How beautiful! The mountains from without
  Listen in silence for the word said next,

(What word will men say?) here where Giotto planted
His campanile, like an unperplexed
Question to Heaven, concerning the things granted
To a great people, who, being greatly vexed
In act, in aspiration keep undaunted!
(What word says God?) The sculptor's Night and Day,
And Dawn and Twilight, wait in marble scorn,
Like dogs couched on a dunghill, on the clay
From whence the Medicean stamp's outworn,—
The final putting off of all such sway
By all such hands, and freeing of the unborn
In Florence, and the world outside his Florence.
That's Michel Angelo! his statues wait
In the small chapel of the dim St. Lawrence!
Day's eyes are breaking bold and passionate

Over his shoulder, and will flash abhorrence
On darkness, and with level looks meet fate,
When once loose from that marble film of theirs:
The Night has wild dreams in her sleep; the Dawn
Is haggard as the sleepless: Twilight wears
A sort of horror: as the veil withdrawn
'Twixt the artist's soul and works had left them heirs
Of the deep thoughts which would not quail nor fawn,
His angers and contempts, his hope and love;
For not without a meaning did he place
Princely Urbino on the seat above
With everlasting shadow on his face;
While the slow dawns and twilights disapprove
The ashes of his long-extinguished race,
Which never shall clog more the feet of men.

IV.

I do believe, divinest Angelo,
That winter-hour, in Via Larga, when
Thou wert commanded to build up in snow
Some marvel of thine art, which straight again
Dissolved beneath the sun's Italian glow,
While thine eyes, still broad with the plastic passion,
Thawed, too, in drops of wounded manhood, . . since,
Mocking alike thine art and indignation,
Laughed at the palace-window the new prince, . .
"Aha! this genius needs for exaltation,
When all's said, and howe'er the proud may wince,
A little marble from our princely mines!"
I do believe that hour thou laughedst too,

For the whole world and for thy Florentines,
After those few tears—which were only few !
That as, beneath the sun, the grand white lines
Of thy snow-statue trembled and withdrew,—
The head, erect as Jove's, being palsied first,
The eyelids flattened, the full brow turned blank,—
When the right hand, upraised as if it cursed,
Dropped, a mere snowball, and the people sank
Their voices, though a louder laughter burst
From the window,—Michel, then, thy soul could thank
God and the prince, for promise and presage,
And laugh the laugh back, I think, verily,
Thine eyes being purged by tears of righteous rage,
To read a wrong into a prophecy,
And measure a true great man's heritage
Against a mere Grand-duke's posterity.

I think thy soul said then, "I do not need
A princedom and its quarries, after all;
For if I write, paint, carve a word, indeed,
On book or board or dust, on floor or wall,
The same is kept of God who taketh heed
That not a letter of the meaning fall,
Or ere it touch and teach His world's deep heart,
Outlasting, therefore, all your lordships, Sir!
So keep your stone, beseech you, for your part,
To cover up your grave-place and refer
The proper titles! *I* live by my art!
The thought I threw into this snow shall stir
This gazing people when their gaze is done;
And the tradition of your act and mine,
When all the snow is melted in the sun,
Shall gather up, for unborn men, a sign

Of what is the true princedom! ay, and none
Shall laugh that day, except the drunk with wine."

V.

Amen, great Angelo! the day is come;
And, if we laugh not on it, shall we weep?
Much more we shall not. Through the mournful hum
Of poets sonneteering in their sleep
'Neath the pale olives, which droop, tickling some
On chin and forehead from a dream too deep,—
Through all that drowsy hum of voices smooth,
The hopeful bird mounts carolling from brake;
The hopeful child, with leaps to catch his growth,
Sings open-eyed for liberty's sweet sake;
And I, who am a singer too, forsooth,
Prefer to sing with these who are awake,

With birds, with babes, with men who will not fear
The baptism of the holy morning dew,
(And many of such wakers now are here,
Complete in their anointed manhood, who
Will greatly dare and greatlier persevere !)
Than join those old thin voices with my new,
And sigh for Italy with some safe sigh
Cooped up in music 'twixt an oh and ah,—
Nay, hand in hand with that young child, will I
Rather go singing "*Bella libertà,*"
Than, with those poets, croon the dead or cry
"*Se tu men bella fossi, Italia !*"

VI.

"Less wretched if less fair," perhaps a truth
Is so far plain in this—that Italy,

Long trammelled with the purple of her youth
Against her age's due activity,
Sate still upon her graves, without the ruth
Of death, but also without energy
And hope of life. "What's Italy?" men ask:
And others answer, "Virgil, Cicero,
Catullus, Cæsar." And what more? to task
The memory closer—"Why, Boccaccio,
Dante, Petrarca,"—and if still the flask
Appears to yield its wine by drops too slow,—
"Angelo, Raffael, Pergolese,"—all
Whose strong hearts beat through stone, or charged, again,
Cloth-threads with fire of souls electrical,
Or broke up heaven for music. What more then?

Why, then, no more. The chaplet's last beads fall
In naming the last saintship within ken,
And, after that, none prayeth in the land.
Alas, this Italy has too long swept
Heroic ashes up for hour-glass sand;
Of her own past, impassioned nympholept!
Consenting to be nailed by the hand
To the same bay-tree under which she stepped
A queen of old, and plucked a leafy branch;
And licensing the world too long, indeed,
To use her broad phylacteries to staunch
And stop her bloody lips, which took no heed
How one quick breath would draw an avalanche
Of living sons around her, to succeed
The vanished generations. Could she count
Those oil-eaters, with large, live, mobile mouths

Agape for maccaroni, in the amount
Of consecrated heroes of her south's
Bright rosary? The pitcher at the fount,
The gift of gods, being broken,—why, one loathes
To let the ground-leaves of the place confer
A natural bowl. And thus, she chose to seem
No nation, but the poet's pensioner,
With alms from every land of song and dream;
While her own pipers sweetly piped of her,
Until their proper breaths, in that extreme
Of sighing, split the reed on which they played!
Of which, no more: but never say "no more"
To Italy! Her memories undismayed
Say rather "evermore"—her graves implore
Her future to be strong and not afraid—
Her very statues send their looks before!

VII.

We do not serve the dead—the past is past!
God lives, and lifts his glorious mornings up
Before the eyes of men, who wake at last,
And put away the meats they used to sup,
And on the dry dust of the ground outcast
The dregs remaining of the ancient cup,
And turn to wakeful prayer and worthy act.
The dead, upon their awful 'vantage ground,—
The sun not in their faces,—shall abstract
No more our strength: we will not be discrowned
Through treasuring their crowns, nor deign transact
A barter of the present, in a sound,
For what was counted good in foregone days.
O Dead, ye shall no longer cling to us

With your stiff hands of desiccating praise,
And hold us backward by the garment thus,
To stay and laud you in long virelays!
Still, no! we will not be oblivious
Of our own lives, because ye lived before,
Nor of our acts, because ye acted well,—
We thank you that ye first unlatched the door—
We will not make it inaccessible
By thankings in the doorway any more,
But will go onward to extinguish hell
With our fresh souls, our younger hope, and God's
Maturity of purpose. Soon shall we
Be the dead too! and, that our periods
Of life may round themselves to memory,
As smoothly as on our graves the funeral-sods,
We must look to it to excel as ye,

And bear our age as far, unlimited
By the last sea-mark! so, to be invoked
By future generations, as the Dead.

VIII.

'Tis true that when the dust of death has choked
A great man's voice, the common words he said
Turn oracles,—the meanings which he yoked
Like horses, draw like griffins!—this is true
And acceptable. Also I desire,
When men make record, with the flowers they strew,
"Savonarola's soul went out in fire
Upon our Grand-duke's piazza, and burned through
A moment first, or ere he did expire,
The veil betwixt the right and wrong, and showed
How near God sate and judged the judges there,—"

Desire, upon the pavement overstrewed,
To cast my violets with as reverent care,
And prove that all the winters which have snowed
Cannot snow out the scent, from stones and air,
Of a sincere man's virtues. This was he,
Savonarola, who, while Peter sank
With his whole boat-load, called courageously
'Wake Christ, wake Christ!"—who, having tried the
tank
Of the church-waters used for baptistry
Ere Luther lived to spill them, said they stank!
Who also, by a princely deathbed, cried
"Loose Florence, or God will not loose thy soul,"
While the Magnificent fell back and died
Beneath the star-looks, shooting from the cowl,
Which turned to wormwood bitterness the wide

Deep sea of his ambitions. It were foul
  To grudge Savonarola and the rest
Their violets! rather pay them quick and fresh!
  The emphasis of death makes manifest
The eloquence of action in our flesh;
  And men who, living, were but dimly guessed,
When once free from their life's entangled mesh,
  Show their full length in graves, or even indeed
Exaggerate their stature, in the flat,
  To noble admirations which exceed
Nobly, nor sin in such excess. For that
  Is wise and righteous. We, who are the seed
Of buried creatures, if we turned and spate
  Upon our antecedents, we were vile.
Bring violets rather! If these had not walked
  Their furlong, could we hope to walk our mile?

Therefore bring violets! Yet if we, self-baulked,
  Stand still a-strewing violets all the while,
These had as well not moved, ourselves not talked
  Of these. So rise up with a cheerful smile,
And, having strewn the violets, reap the corn,
  And, having reaped and garnered, bring the
    plough
And draw new furrows 'neath the healthy morn,
  And plant the great Hereafter in this Now.

IX.

Of old 'twas so. How step by step was worn,
  As each man gained on each, securely!—how
Each by his own strength sought his own ideal,
  The ultimate Perfection leaning bright
From out the sun and stars, to bless the leal

And earnest search of all for Fair and Right,
Through the dim forms, by earth accounted real!
Because old Jubal blew into delight
The souls of men, with clear-piped melodies,
What if young Asaph were content at most
To draw from Jubal's grave, with listening eyes,
Traditionary music's floating ghost
Into the grass-grown silence? were it wise?
Is it not wiser, Jubal's breath being lost,
That Miriam clashed her cymbals to surprise
The sun between her white arms flung apart,
With new, glad, golden sounds? that David's strings
O'erflowed his hand with music from his heart?
So harmony grows full from many springs,
And happy accident turns holy art.

X.

Or enter, in your Florence wanderings,
Santa Maria Novella church. You pass
The left stair, where, at plague-time, Macchiavel
Saw one with set fair face as in a glass,
Dressed out against the fear of death and hell,
Rustling her silks in pauses of the mass,
To keep the thought off how her husband fell,
When she left home, stark dead across her feet—
The stair leads up to what Orgagna gave
Of Dante's dæmons; but you, passing it,
Ascend the right stair of the farther nave,
To muse in a small chapel scarcely lit
By Cimabue's Virgin. Bright and brave,
That picture was accounted, mark, of old!

A king stood bare before its sovran grace;
  A reverent people shouted to behold
The picture, not the king; and even the place
  Containing such a miracle, grew bold,
Named the Glad Borgo from that beauteous face,
  Which thrilled the artist, after work, to think
That his ideal Mary-smile should stand
  So very near him!—he, within the brink
Of all that glory, let in by his hand
  With too divine a rashness! Yet none shrink
Who gaze here now—albeit the thing is planned
  Sublimely in the thought's simplicity.
The Virgin, throned in empyreal state,
  Minds only the young babe upon her knee;
While, each side, angels bear the royal weight,
  Prostrated meekly, smiling tenderly

Oblivion of their wings! the Child thereat
  Stretches its hand like God. If any should,
Because of some stiff draperies and loose joints,
  Gaze scorn down from the heights of Raffaelhood,
On Cimabue's picture,—Heaven anoints
  The head of no such critic, and his blood
The poet's curse strikes full on, and appoints
  To ague and cold spasms for evermore.
A noble picture! worthy of the shout
  Wherewith along the streets the people bore
Its cherub faces, which the sun threw out
  Until they stooped and entered the church door!—
Yet rightly was young Giotto talked about,
  Whom Cimabue found among the sheep,
And knew, as gods know gods, and carried home
  To paint the things he painted, with a deep

And fuller insight, and so overcome
  His chapel-Virgin with a heavenlier sweep
Of light. For thus we mount into the sum
  Of great things known or acted. I hold, too,
That Cimabue smiled upon the lad,
  At the first stroke which passed what he could do,—
Or else his Virgin's smile had never had
  Such sweetness in 't. All great men who foreknew
Their heirs in art, for art's sake have been glad,
  And bent their old white heads as if uncrowned,
Fanatics of their pure ideals still,
  Far more than of their laurels which were found
With some less stalwart struggle of the will.
  If old Margheritone trembled, swooned,
And died despairing at the open sill
  Of other men's achievements, (who achieved,

By loving art beyond the master!) he
  Was old Margheritone and conceived
Never, at youngest and most ecstasy,
  A Virgin like that dream of one, which heaved
The death-sigh from his heart. If wistfully
  Margheritone sickened at the smell
Of Cimabue's laurel, let him go!—
  Strong Cimabue stood up very well
In spite of Giotto's—and Angelico,
  The artist-saint, kept smiling in his cell
The smile with which he welcomed the sweet slow
  Inbreak of angels, (whitening through the dim
That he might paint them!) while the sudden sense
  Of Raffael's future was revealed to him
By force of his own fair works' competence.
  The same blue waters where the dolphins swim

Suggest the Tritons. Through the blue Immense,
  Strike out all swimmers! cling not in the way
Of one another, so to sink; but learn
  The strong man's impulse, catch the fresh'ning
      spray
He throws up in his motions, and discern
  By his clear, westering eye, the time of day.
O God, thou hast set us worthy gifts to earn,
  Beside thy heaven and Thee! and when I say
'Tis worth while for the weakest man alive
  To live and die,—there 's room too, I repeat,
For all the strongest to live well, and strive
  Their own way, by their individual heat,
Like a new bee-swarm leaving the old hive
  Despite the wax which tempteth violet-sweet.
So let the living live, the dead retain

Flowers on cold graves! — though honour's best
supplied,
When we bring actions, to prove their's not vain.

XI.

Cold graves, we say? it shall be testified
That living men who throb in heart and train,
Without the dead, were colder. If we tried
To sink the past beneath our feet, be sure
The future would not stand. Precipitate
This old roof from the shrine—and, insecure,
The nesting swallows fly off, mate from mate.
Scant were the gardens, if the graves were fewer!
And the green poplars grew no longer straight,
Whose tops not looked to Troy. Why, who would fight
For Athens, and not swear by Marathon?

Who would build temples, without tombs in sight?
  Who live, without some dead man's benison?
Who seek truth, hope for good, or strive for right,
  If, looking up, he saw not in the sun
Some angel of the martyrs, all day long
  Standing and waiting! your last rhythms will need
The earliest key-note. Could I sing this song,
  If my dead masters had not taken heed
To help the heavens and earth to make me strong,
  As the wind ever will find out some reed,
And touch it to such issues as belong
  To such a frail thing? Who denies the dead,
Libations from full cups? Unless we choose
  To look back to the hills behind us spread,
The plains before us sadden and confuse;
  If orphaned, we are disinherited.

XII.

I would but turn these lachrymals to use,
Fill them with fresh oil from the olive grove,
To feed the new lamp fuller. Shall I say
What made my heart beat with exulting love,
A few weeks back?

XIII.

. . . . The day was such a day
As Florence owes the sun. The sky above,
Its weight upon the mountains seemed to lay,
And palpitate in glory, like a dove
Who has flown too fast, full-hearted. Take away
The image! for the heart of man beat higher
That day in Florence, flooding all her streets

And piazzas with a tumult and desire.
The people, with accumulated heats,
And faces turned one way, as if one fire
Did draw and flush them, leaving their old beats,
Went upward to the palace Pitti wall,
To thank their Grand-duke, who, not quite of course,
Had graciously permitted, at their call,
The citizens to use their civic force
To guard their civic homes. So, one and all,
The Tuscan cities streamed up to the source
Of this new good, at Florence; taking it
As good so far, presageful of more good,—
The first torch of Italian freedom, lit
To toss in the next tiger's face who should
Approach too near them in a cruel fit,—
The first pulse of an even flow of blood,

To prove the level of Italian veins
Toward rights perceived and granted. How we gazed
From Casa Guidi windows, while, in trains
Of orderly procession—banners raised,
And intermittent bursts of martial strains
Which died upon the shout, as if amazed
By gladness beyond music—they passed on!
The magistrates, with their insignia, passed;
And all the people shouted in the sun,
And all the thousand windows which had cast
A ripple of silks, in blue and scarlet, down,
As if the houses overflowed at last,
Seemed to grow larger with fair heads and eyes.
The lawyers passed; and still arose the shout,
And hands broke from the windows, to surprise
Those grave calm brows with bay-tree leaves thrown out.

The priesthood passed: the friars, with worldly-wise
Keen, sidelong glances from their beards, about
The street, to see who shouted! many a monk
Who takes a long rope in the waist, was there!
Whereat the popular exultation drunk
With indrawn "vivas," the whole sunny air,
While through the murmuring windows rose and sunk
A cloud of kerchiefed hands! "the church makes fair
Her welcome in the new Pope's name." Ensued
The black sign of the "martyrs!" name no name,
But count the graves in silence. Next, were viewed
The artists; next, the trades; and after came
The populace, with flag and rights as good;
And very loud the shout was for that same
Motto, "Il popolo," IL POPOLO,—
The word meant dukedom, empire, majesty,

And kings in such an hour might read it so.
And next, with banners, each in his degree,
Deputed representatives a-row,
Of every separate state of Tuscany:
Siena's she-wolf, bristling on the fold
Of the first flag, preceded Pisa's hare;
And Massa's lion floated calm in gold,
Pienza's following with his silver stare;
Arezzo's steed pranced clear from bridle-hold,—
And well might shout our Florence, greeting there
These, and more brethren! Last, the world had sent
The various children of her teeming flanks—
Greeks, English, French—as to some parliament
Of lovers of her Italy, in ranks,
Each bearing its land's symbols reverent;
At which the stones seemed breaking into thanks

And rattling up to the sky, such sounds in proof
Arose! the very house-walls seemed to bend,
The very windows, up from door to roof,
Flashed out a rapture of bright heads, to mend,
With passionate looks, the gesture's whirling off
A hurricane of leaves! Three hours did end
While all these passed; and ever in the crowd,
Rude men, unconscious of the tears that kept
Their beards moist, shouted; and some laughed aloud,
And none asked any why they laughed and wept:
Friends kissed each other's cheeks, and foes long vowed
Did it more warmly; two-months' babies leapt
Right upward in their mother's arms, whose black,
Wide, glittering eyes looked elsewhere; lovers pressed
Each before either, neither glancing back;

And peasant maidens, smoothly 'tired and tressed,
Forgot to finger on their throats the slack
Great pearl-strings ; while old blind men would not rest,
But pattered with their staves and with their shoes
Still on the stones, and smiled as if they saw.
O Heaven ! I think that day had noble use
Among God's days. So near stood Right and Law,
Both mutually forborne ! Law would not bruise,
Nor Right deny ; and each in reverent awe
Honoured the other. What if, ne'ertheless,
The sun did, that day, leave upon the vines
No charta, and the liberal Duke's excess
Did scarce exceed a Guelf's or Ghibelline's
In the specific actual righteousness
Of what that day he granted ;* still the signs

* Since when the constitutional concessions have been complete in Tuscany, as all the world knows. The event breaks in upon the meditation, and is too fast for prophecy in these strange times.—E. B. B.

Are good, and full of promise, we must say,
When multitudes thank kings for granting prayers,
And kings concede their people's right to pray,
Both in the sunshine! Griefs are not despairs,
So uttered; nor can royal claims dismay,
When men, from humble homes and ducal chairs,
Hate wrong together. It was well to view
Those banners ruffled in a Grand-duke's face,
Inscribed, "Live freedom, union, and all true
Brave patriots who are aided by God's grace!"
Nor was it ill, when Leopoldo drew
His little children to the window-place
He stood in at the Pitti, to suggest
They, too, should govern as the people willed.
What a cry rose then! some, who saw the best,

Sware that his eyes filled up, and overfilled
With good warm human tears, which unre-
pressed
Ran down. I like his face: the forehead's build
Has no capacious genius, yet perhaps
Sufficient comprehension,—mild and sad,
And careful nobly,—not with care that wraps
Self-loving hearts, to stifle and make mad,
But careful with the care that shuns a lapse
Of faith and duty,—studious not to add
A burden in the gathering of a gain.
And so, God save the Duke, I say with those
Who that day shouted it, and while dukes reign,
May all wear, in the visible overflows
Of spirit, such a look of careful pain!
Methinks God loves it better than repose.

XIV.

And all the people who went up to let
Their hearts out to that Duke, as has been told—
Where guess ye that the living people met,
Kept tryst, formed ranks, chose leaders, first unrolled
Their banners?
In the Loggia? where is set
Cellini's godlike Perseus, bronze—or gold—
(How name the metal, when the statue flings
Its soul so in your eyes?) with brow and sword
Superbly calm, as all opposing things
Slain with the Gorgon, were no more abhorred
Since ended?
No! the people sought no wings
From Perseus in the Loggia, nor implored

An inspiration in the place beside,
  From that dim bust of Brutus, jagged and grand,
Where Buonarotti passionately tried
  Out of the clenched marble to demand
The head of Rome's sublimest homicide,
  Then dropt the quivering mallet from his hand,
Despairing he could find no model stuff
  Of Brutus, in all Florence, where he found
The gods and gladiators thick enough?
  Not there! the people chose still holier ground!
The people, who are simple, blind, and rough,
  Know their own angels, after looking round.
What chose they then? where met they?

XV.

On the stone
  Call'd Dante's,—a plain flat stone, scarce discerned

From others in the pavement,—whereupon
 He used to bring his quiet chair out, turned
To Brunelleschi's church, and pour alone
 The lava of his spirit when it burned—
It is not cold to-day. O passionate
 Poor Dante, who, a banished Florentine,
Didst sit austere at banquets of the great,
 And muse upon this far-off stone of thine,
And think how oft the passers used to wait
 A moment, in the golden day's decline,
With "good night, dearest Dante!"—well, good night!
 I muse now, Dante, and think, verily,
Though chapelled in Ravenna's byeway, might
 Thy buried bones be thrilled to ecstasy,
Could'st know thy favourite stone's elected right
 As tryst-place for thy Tuscans to foresee

Their earliest chartas from! good night, good morn,
  Henceforward, Dante! now my soul is sure
That thine is better comforted of scorn,
  And looks down from the stars in fuller cure,
Than when, in Santa Croce church, forlorn
  Of any corpse, the architect and hewer
Did pile the empty marbles as thy tomb!
  For now thou art no longer exiled, now
Best honoured!—we salute thee who art come
  Back to the old stone with a softer brow
Than Giotto drew upon the wall, for some
  Good lovers of our age to track and plough
Their way to, through Time's ordures stratified,
  And startle broad awake into the dull
Bargello chamber. Now, thou 'rt milder eyed,
  And Beatrix may leap up glad to cull

Thy first smile, even in heaven and at her side,
 Like that which, nine years old, looked beautiful
At Tuscan May-game. Foolish words! I meant
 Only that Dante loved his Florence well,
And Florence, now, to love him is content!
 I mean too, certes, that the sweetest smell
Of love's dear incense, by the living sent
 To find the dead, is not accessible
To your low livers! no narcotic,—not
 Swung in a censer to a sleepy tune,—
But trod out in the morning air, by hot
 Quick spirits, who tread firm to ends foreshown,
And use the name of greatness unforgot,
 To meditate what greatness may be done.

XVI.

For Dante sits in heaven, and ye stand here,
And more remains for doing, all must feel,
Than trysting on his stone from year to year
To shift processions, civic heel to heel,
The town's thanks to the Pitti. Are ye freer
For what was felt that day? A chariot wheel
May spin fast, yet the chariot never roll.
But if that day suggested something good,
And bettered, with one purpose, soul by soul,—
Better means freer. A land's brotherhood
Is most puissant! Men, upon the whole,
Are what they can be,—nations, what they would.

XVII.

Will, therefore, to be strong, thou Italy!

Will to be noble! Austrian Metternich
Can fix no yoke unless the neck agree;
And thine is like the lion's when the thick
Dews shudder from it, and no man would be
The stroker of his mane, much less would prick
His nostril with a reed. When nations roar
Like lions, who shall tame them, and defraud
Of the due pasture by the river-shore?
Roar, therefore! shake your dew-laps dry abroad.
The amphitheatre with open door
Leads back upon the benches who applaud
The last spear-thruster!

XVIII.

Yet the Heavens forbid
That we should call on passion to confront

The brutal with the brutal, and, amid
 This ripening world, suggest a lion-hunt
And lion-vengeance for the wrongs men did
 And do now, though the spears are getting blunt.
We only call, because the sight and proof
 Of lion-strength hurts nothing; and to show
A lion-heart, and measure paw with hoof,
 Helps something, even, and will instruct a foe
Well as the onslaught, how to stand aloof!
 Or else the world gets past the mere brute blow
Given or taken. Children use the fist
 Until they are of age to use the brain:
And so we needed Cæsars to assist
 Man's justice, and Napoleons to explain
God's counsel, when a point was nearly missed,
 Until our generations should attain

Christ's stature nearer. Not that we, alas!
  Attain already; but a single inch
Will help to look down on the swordsman's pass,
  As Roland on a coward who could flinch;
And, after chloroform and ether-gas,
  We find out slowly what the bee and finch
Have ready found, through Nature's lamp in each,—
  How to our races we may justify
Our individual claims, and, as we reach
  Our own grapes, bend the top vines to supply
The children's uses: how to fill a breach
  With olive branches; how to quench a lie
With truth, and smite a foe upon the cheek
  With Christ's most conquering kiss! why, these are
    things
Worth a great nation's finding, to prove weak

The "glorious arms" of military kings!
And so with wide embrace, my England, seek
To stifle the bad heat and flickerings
Of this world's false and nearly expended fire!
Draw palpitating arrows to the wood,
And send abroad thy high hopes, and thy higher
Resolves, from that most virtuous altitude,
Till nations shall unconsciously aspire
By looking up to thee, and learn that good
And glory are not different. Announce law
By freedom; exalt chivalry by peace;
Instruct how clear calm eyes can overawe,
And how pure hands, stretched simply to release
A bond-slave, will not need a sword to draw
To be held dreadful. O my England, crease
Thy purple with no alien agonies

Which reach thee through the net of war! No war!
Disband thy captains, change thy victories,
Be henceforth prosperous as the angels are—
Helping, not humbling.

XIX.

Drums and battle cries
Go out in music of the morning star—
And soon we shall have thinkers in the place
Of fighters; each found able as a man
To strike electric influence through a race,
Unstayed by city-wall and barbican.
The poet shall look grander in the face
Than ever he looked of old, when he began
To sing that "Achillean wrath which slew
So many heroes,"—seeing he shall treat

The deeds of souls heroic toward the true—
  The oracles of life—previsions sweet
And awful, like divine swans gliding through
  White arms of Ledas, which will leave the heat
Of their escaping godship to endue
  The human medium with a heavenly flush.
Meanwhile, in this same Italy we want
  Not popular passion, to arise and crush,
But popular conscience, which may covenant
  For what it knows. Concede without a blush—
To grant the "civic guard" is not to grant
  The civic spirit, living and awake.
Those lappets on your shoulders, citizens,
  Your eyes strain after sideways till they ache,
While still, in admirations and amens,
  The crowd comes up on festa-days, to take

The great sight in—are not intelligence,
  Not courage even—alas, if not the sign
Of something very noble, they are nought;
  For every day ye dress your sallow kine
With fringes down their cheeks, though unbesought
  They loll their heavy heads and drag the wine,
And bear the wooden yoke as they were taught
  The first day. What ye want is light—indeed
Not sunlight—(ye may well look up surprised
  To those unfathomable heavens that feed
Your purple hills!)—but God's light organised
  In some high soul, crowned capable to lead
The conscious people,—conscious and advised,—
  For if we lift a people like mere clay,
It falls the same. We want thee, O unfound
  And sovran teacher!—if thy beard be grey

Or black, we bid thee rise up from the ground
  And speak the word God giveth thee to say,
Inspiring into all this people round,
  Instead of passion, thought, which pioneers
All generous passion, purifies from sin,
  And strikes the hour for. Rise thou teacher! here 's
A crowd to make a nation!—best begin
  By making each a man, till all be peers
Of earth's true patriots and pure martyrs in
  Knowing and daring. Best unbar the doors
Which Peter's heirs keep locked so overclose
  They only let the mice across the floors,
While every churchman dangles as he goes
  The great key at his girdle, and abhors
In Christ's name, meekly. Open wide the house—
  Concede the entrance with Christ's liberal mind,

And set the tables with His wine and bread.
  What! commune in "both kinds?" In every kind—
Wine, wafer, love, hope, truth, unlimited,
  Nothing kept back. For, when a man is blind
To starlight, will he see the rose is red?
  A bondsman shivering at a Jesuit's foot—
"Væ! meâ culpâ!" is not like to stand
  A freedman at a despot's, and dispute
His titles by the balance in his hand,
  Weighing them "suo jure." Tend the root,
If careful of the branches; and expand
  The inner souls of men, before you strive
For civic heroes.

XX.

But the teacher, where?

From all these crowded faces, all alive,—
Eyes, of their own lids flashing themselves bare,—
And brows that with a mobile life contrive
A deeper shadow,—may we no wise dare
To point a finger out, and touch a man,
And cry "this is the leader." What, all these!—
Broad heads, black eyes,—yet not a soul that ran
From God down with a message? All, to please
The donna waving measures with her fan,
And not the judgment-angel on his knees—
The trumpet just an inch off from his lips—
Who when he breathes next, will put out the sun?
Yet mankind's self were foundered in eclipse,
If lacking, with a great work to be done,
A doer. No, the earth already dips
Back into light—a better day's begun—

And soon this doer, teacher, will stand plain,
And build the golden pipes and synthesize
This people-organ for a holy strain:
And we who hope thus, still in all these eyes,
Go sounding for the deep look which shall drain
Suffused thought into channelled enterprise!
Where is the teacher? What now may he do,
Who shall do greatly? Doth he gird his waist
With a monk's rope, like Luther? or pursue
The goat, like Tell? or dry his nets in haste,
Like Masaniello when the sky was blue?
Keep house like any peasant, with inlaced,
Bare, brawny arms about his favourite child,
And meditative looks beyond the door.—
(But not to mark the kidling's teeth have filed
The green shoots of his vine which last year bore

Full twenty bunches;) or, on triple-piled
Throne-velvets, shall we see him bless the poor,
Like any Pontiff, in the Poorest's name,—
While the tiara holds itself aslope
Upon his steady brows, which, all the same,
Bend mildly to permit the people's hope?

XXI.

Whatever hand shall grasp this oriflamme,
Whatever man (last peasant or first Pope
Seeking to free his country!) shall appear,
Teach, lead, strike fire into the masses, fill
These empty bladders with fine air, insphere
These wills into a unity of will,
And make of Italy a nation—dear
And blessed be that man! the Heavens shall kill

No leaf the earth shall grow for him; and Death
Shall cast him back upon the lap of Life,
To live more surely, in a clarion-breath
Of hero-music! Brutus, with the knife,
Rienzi, with the fasces, throb beneath
Rome's stones; and more, who threw away joy's fife
Like Pallas, that the beauty of their souls
Might ever shine untroubled and entire!
But if it can be true that he who rolls
The Church's thunders will reserve her fire
For only light; from eucharistic bowls
Will pour new life for nations that expire,
And rend the scarlet of his Papal vest
To gird the weak loins of his countrymen—
I hold that man surpasses all the rest
Of Romans, heroes, patriots,—and that when

He sat down on the throne, he dispossessed
The first graves of some glory. See again,
This country-saving is a glorious thing!
Why, say a common man achieved it? Well!
Say, a rich man did? Excellent! A king?
That grows sublime! A priest? Improbable!
A Pope? Ah, there we stop and cannot bring
Our faith up to the leap, with history's bell
So heavy round the neck of it—albeit
We fain would grant the possibility
For *thy* sake, Pio Nono!

XXII.

Stretch thy feet
In that case—I will kiss them reverently
As any pilgrim to the Papal seat!

And, such proved possible, thy throne to me
  Shall seem as holy a place as Pellico's
Venetian dungeon; or as Spielberg's grate,
  Where the fair Lombard woman hung the
      rose
Of her sweet soul, by its own dewy weight,
  (Because her sun shone *inside* to the close!)
And pining so, died early, yet too late
  For what she suffered! Yea, I will not choose
Betwixt thy throne, Pope Pius, and the spot
  Marked red for ever spite of rains and dews,
Where two fell riddled by the Austrian's shot—
  The brothers Bandiera, who accuse,
With one same mother-voice and face (that what
  They speak may be invincible), the sins
Of earth's tormentors before God, the just,

Until the unconscious thunder-bolt begins
To loosen in His grasp.

XXIII.

And yet we must
Beware, and mark the natural kiths and kins
Of circumstance and office, and distrust
A rich man reasoning in a poor man's hut
A poet who neglects pure truth to prove
Statistic fact; a child who leaves a rut
For the smooth road; a priest who vows his
glove
Exhales no grace; a prince who walks a-foot;
A woman who has sworn she will not love;
Ninth Pius sitting in Seventh Gregory's chair,
With Andrea Doria's forehead!

XXIV.

Count what goes
To making up a Pope, before he wear
That triple crown. We pass the world-wide throes
Which went to make the Popedom,—the despair
Of free men, good men, wise men; the dread shows
Of women's faces, by the faggot's flash,
Tossed out, to the minutest stir and throb
Of the white lips, least tremble of a lash,
To glut the red stare of the licensed mob!
The short mad cries down oubliettes,—the plash
So horribly far off! priests, trained to rob;
And kings that, like encouraged nightmares, sate
On nations' hearts most heavily distressed
With monstrous sights and apophthegms of fate.

We pass these things,—because "the times" are prest
With necessary charges of the weight
Of all the sin; and "Calvin, for the rest,
Made bold to burn Servetus—Ah, men err!"—
And, so do *Churches!* which is all we mean
To bring to proof in any register
Of theological fat kine and lean—
So drive them back into the pens! refer
Old sins with long beards, and "I wis and ween,"
Entirely to the times—the times—the times!
Nor ever ask why this preponderant,
Infallible, pure Church could set her chimes
Most loudly then, just then; most jubilant,
Precisely then—when mankind stood in crimes
Full heart-deep, and Heaven's judgments were not scant.

Inquire still less, what signifies a Church
Of perfect inspiration and pure laws,
Who burns the first man with a brimstone torch,
And grinds the second, bone by bone, because
The times, forsooth, are used to rack and scorch!
What *is* a holy Church, unless she awes
The times down from their sins? Did Christ select
Such amiable times, to come and teach
Love to, and mercy? Why, the world were wrecked,
If every mere great man, who lives to reach
A little leaf of popular respect,
Attained not simply by some special breach
In his land's customs,—by some precedence
In thought and act—which, having proved him higher
Than his own times, proved too his competence
Of helping them to wonder and aspire.

XXV.

My words are guiltless of the bigot's sense!
My soul has fire to mingle with the fire
Of all these souls, within or out of doors
Of Rome's Church or another. I believe
In one priest, and one temple, with its floors
Of shining jasper, gloom'd at morn and eve
By countless knees of earnest auditors;
And crystal walls, too lucid to perceive,—
That none may take the measure of the place
And say, "so far the porphyry; then, the flint—
To this mark, mercy goes, and there, ends grace,"
While still the permeable crystals hint
At some white starry distance, bathed in space!
I feel how nature's ice-crusts keep the dint

Ofundersprings of silent Deity;
I hold the articulated gospels, which
Show Christ among us, crucified on tree;
I love all who love truth, if poor or rich
In what they have won of truth possessively!
No altars and no hands defiled with pitch
Shall scare me off, but I will pray and eat
With all these—taking leave to choose my ewers
And say at last, "Your visible Churches cheat
Their inward types; and if a Church assures
Of standing without failure and defeat,
That Church both fails and lies!"

XXVI.

To leave which lures
Of wider subject through past years,—behold,

We come back from the Popedom to the Pope,
  To ponder what he *must* be, ere we are bold
For what he *may* be, with our heavy hope
  To trust upon his soul. So, fold by fold,
Explore this mummy in the priestly cope
  Transmitted through the darks of time, to catch
The man within the wrappage, and discern
  How he, an honest man, upon the watch
Full fifty years, for what a man may learn,
  Contrived to get just there; with what a snatch
Of old world oboli he had to earn
  The passage through; with what a drowsy sop
To drench the busy barkings of his brain;
  What ghosts of pale tradition, wreathed with hop
'Gainst wakeful thought, he had to entertain
  For heavenly visions; and consent to stop

The clock at noon, and let the hour remain
  (Without vain windings up) inviolate,
Against all chimings from the belfry. Lo!
  From every given pope, you must abate,
Albeit you love him, some things—good, you know—
  Which every given heretic you hate
Claims for his own, as being plainly so.
  A pope must hold by popes a little,—yes,
By councils,—from Nicæa up to Trent,—
  By hierocratic empire, more or less
Irresponsible to men,—he must resent
  Each man's particular conscience, and repress
Inquiry, meditation, argument,
  As tyrants faction. Also, he must not
Love truth too dangerously, but prefer
  "The interests of the Church," because a blot

Is better than a rent in miniver,—
  Submit to see the people swallow hot
Husk-porridge which his chartered churchmen stir
  Quoting the only true God's epigraph,
"Feed my lambs, Peter!"—must consent to sit
  Attesting with his pastoral ring and staff,
To such a picture of our Lady, hit
  Off well by artist angels, though not half
As fair as Giotto would have painted it;
  To such a vial, where a dead man's blood
Runs yearly warm beneath a churchman's finger;
  To such a holy house of stone and wood,
Whereof a cloud of angels was the bringer
  From Bethlehem to Loreto!—Were it good
For any pope on earth to be a flinger
  Of stones against these high-niched counterfeits?

Apostates only are iconoclasts.
He dares not say, while this false thing abets
That true thing, "this is false!" he keepeth fasts
And prayers, as prayers and fasts were silver frets
To change a note upon a string that lasts,
And make a lie a virtue. Now, if he
Did more than this,—higher hoped and braver dared,—
I think he were a pope in jeopardy,
Or no pope rather! for his soul had barred
The vaulting of his life. And certainly,
If he do only this, mankind's regard
Moves on from him at once, to seek some new
Teacher and leader! He is good and great
According to the deeds a pope can do;
Most liberal, save those bonds; affectionate,
As princes may be; and, as priests are, true—

But only the ninth Pius after eight,
  When all 's praised most. At best and hopefullest,
He 's pope—we want a man! his heart beats warm,
  But, like the prince enchanted to the waist,
He sits in stone, and hardens by a charm
  Into the marble of his throne high-placed!
Mild benediction, waves his saintly arm—
  So good! but what we want 's a perfect man,
Complete and all alive: half travertine
  Half suits our need, and ill subserves our plan.
Feet, knees, nerves, sinews, energies divine
  Were never yet too much for men who ran
In such exalted ways as this of thine,
  Deliverer whom we seek, whoe'er thou art,
Pope, prince, or peasant! If, indeed, the first,
  The noblest, therefore! since the heroic heart

Within thee must be great enough to burst
Those trammels buckling to the baser part
Thy saintly peers in Rome, who crossed and cursed
With the same finger.

XXVII.

Come, appear, be found,
If pope or peasant, come! we hear the cock,
The courtier of the mountains when first crowned
With golden dawn; and orient glories flock
To meet the sun upon the highest ground.
Take voice and work! we wait to hear thee knock
At some one of our Florentine nine gates,
On each of which was imaged a sublime
Face of a Tuscan genius, which, for hate's
And love's sake both, our Florence in her prime

Turned boldly on all comers to her states,
As heroes turned their shields in antique time,
Blazoned with honourable acts. And though
The gates are blank now of such images,
And Petrarch looks no more from Nicolo
Toward dear Arezzo, 'twixt the acacia trees,
Nor Dante, from gate Gallo—still we know,
Despite the razing of the blazonries,
Remains the consecration of the shield,—
The dead heroic faces will start out
On all these gates, if foes should take the field,
And blend sublimely, at the earliest shout,
With our live fighters, who will scorn to yield
A hair's-breadth ev'n, when, gazing round about,
They find in what a glorious company
They fight the foes of Florence! Who will grudge

His one poor life, when that great man we see,
Has given five hundred years, the world being judge,
To help the glory of his Italy?
Who, born the fair side of the Alps, will budge,
When Dante stays, when Ariosto stays,
When Petrarch stays, for ever? Ye bring swords,
My Tuscans? Why, if wanted in this haze,
Bring swords, but first bring souls!—bring thoughts and words
Unrusted by a tear of yesterday's,
Yet awful by its wrong, and cut these cords
And mow this green lush falseness to the roots,
And shut the mouth of hell below the swathe!
And if ye can bring songs too, let the lute's
Recoverable music softly bathe
Some poet's hand, that, through all bursts and bruits

Of popular passion—all unripe and rathe
  Convictions of the popular intellect—
Ye may not lack a finger up the air,
  Annunciative, reproving, pure, erect,
To show which way your first Ideal bare
  The whiteness of its wings, when, sorely pecked
By falcons on your wrists, it unaware
  Arose up overhead, and out of sight.

XXVIII.

Meanwhile, let all the far ends of the world
  Breathe back the deep breath of their old delight,
To swell the Italian banner just unfurled.
  Help, lands of Europe! for, if Austria fight,
The drums will bar your slumber. Who had curled
  The laurel for your thousand artists' brows,

If these Italian hands had planted none?
  And who can sit down idle in the house,
Nor hear appeals from Buonarotti's stone
  And Raffael's canvas, rousing and to rouse?
Where 's Poussin's master? Gallic Avignon
  Bred Laura, and Vaucluse's fount has stirred
The heart of France too strongly,—as it lets
  Its little stream out, like a wizard's bird
Which bounds upon its emerald wings, and wets
  The rocks on each side—that she should not gird
Her loins with Charlemagne's sword, when foes beset
  The country of her Petrarch. Spain may well
Be minded how from Italy she caught,
  To mingle with her tinkling Moorish bell,
A fuller cadence and a subtler thought;
  And even the New World, the receptacle

Of freemen, may send glad men, as it ought,
  To greet Vespucci Amerigo's door;
While England claims, by trump of poetry,
  Verona, Venice, the Ravenna shore,
And dearer holds her Milton's Fiesole
  Than Malvern with a sunset running o'er.

XXIX.

And Vallombrosa, we two went to see
  Last June, beloved companion,—where sublime
The mountains live in holy families,
  And the slow pinewoods ever climb and climb
Half up their breasts; just stagger as they seize
  Some grey crag—drop back with it many a time,
And straggle blindly down the precipice!
  The Vallombrosan brooks were strewn as thick

That June-day, knee-deep, with dead beechen leaves,
  As Milton saw them ere his heart grew sick,
And his eyes blind. I think the monks and beeves
  Are all the same too: scarce they have changed the wick
On good St. Gualbert's altar, which receives
  The convent's pilgrims; and the pool in front
Wherein the hill-stream trout are cast, to wait
  The beatific vision, and the grunt
Used at refectory, keeps its weedy state,
  To baffle saintly abbots, who would count
The fish across their breviary, nor 'bate
  The measure of their steps. O waterfalls
And forests! sound and silence! mountains bare,
  That leap up peak by peak, and catch the palls
Of purple and silver mist, to rend and share
  With one another, at electric calls

Of life in the sunbeams,—till we cannot dare
  Fix your shapes, learn your number! we must think
Your beauty and your glory helped to fill
  The cup of Milton's soul so to the brink,
That he no more was thirsty when God's will
  Had shattered to his sense the last chain-link
By which he drew from Nature's visible
  The fresh well-water. Satisfied by this,
He sang of Adam's paradise and smiled,
  Remembering Vallombrosa. Therefore is
The place divine to English man and child—
  We all love Italy.

XXX.

Our Italy 's
The darling of the earth—the treasury, piled

With reveries of gentle ladies, flung
Aside, like ravelled silk, from life's worn stuff—
With coins of scholars' fancy, which, being rung
On work-day counter, still sound silver-proof—
In short, with all the dreams of dreamers young,
Before their heads have time for slipping off
Hope's pillow to the ground. How oft, indeed,
We all have sent our souls out from the north,
On bare white feet which would not print nor bleed,
To climb the Alpine passes and look forth,
Where the low murmuring Lombard rivers lead
Their bee-like way to gardens almost worth
The sight which thou and I see afterward
From Tuscan Bellosguardo, wide awake,
When standing on the actual, blessed sward
Where Galileo stood at nights to take

The vision of the stars, we find it hard,
Gazing upon the earth and heaven, to make
A choice of beauty. Therefore let us all
In England, or in any other land
Refreshed once by the fountain-rise and fall
Of dreams of this fair south,—who understand
A little how the Tuscan musical
Vowels do round themselves, as if they plann'd
Eternities of separate sweetness,—we
Who loved Sorrento vines in picture-book,
Or ere in wine-cup we pledged faith or glee—
Who loved Rome's wolf, with demi-gods at suck,
Or ere we loved truth's own divinity,—
Who loved, in brief, the classic hill and brook,
And Ovid's dreaming tales, and Petrarch's song,
Or ere we loved Love's self!—why, let us give

The blessing of our souls, and wish them strong
To bear it to the height where prayers arrive,
When faithful spirits pray against a wrong;
To this great cause of southern men, who strive
In God's name for man's rights, and shall not fail!

XXXI.

Behold, they shall not fail. The shouts ascend
Above the shrieks, in Naples, and prevail.
Rows of shot corpses, waiting for the end
Of burial, seem to smile up straight and pale
Into the azure air, and apprehend
That final gun-flash from Palermo's coast,
Which lightens their apocalypse of death.
So let them die! The world shows nothing lost;
Therefore, not blood! Above or underneath,

What matter, brothers, if we keep our post
Or truth's and duty's side? As sword to sheath,
Dust turns to grave, but souls find place in Heaven.
O friends, heroic daring is success,
The eucharistic bread requires no leaven;
And though your ends were hopeless, we should bless
Your cause as holy! Strive—and, having striven,
Take, for God's recompense, that righteousness!

PART II.

I.

I WROTE a meditation and a dream,
Hearing a little child sing in the street
I leant upon his music as a theme,
Till it gave way beneath my heart's full beat,
Which tried at an exultant prophecy
But dropped before the measure was complete—
Alas, for songs and hearts! O Tuscany,
O Dante's Florence, is the type too plain?
Didst thou, too, only sing of liberty,
As little children take up a high strain
With unintentioned voices, and break off

To sleep upon their mothers' knees again?
Could'st thou not watch one hour? Then, sleep enough—
That sleep may hasten manhood, and sustain
The faint pale spirit with some muscular stuff.

II.

But we, who cannot slumber as thou dost,
We thinkers, who have thought for thee and failed,—
We hopers, who have hoped for thee and lost,—
We poets, wandered round by dreams,* who hailed
From this Atrides' roof (with lintel-post
Which still drips blood,—the worse part hath prevailed)
The fire-voice of the beacons, to declare
Troy taken, sorrow ended,—cozened through

* Referring to the well-known opening passage of the Agamemnon of Æschylus.

A crimson sunset in a misty air,—
What now remains for such as we, to do?
—God's judgments, peradventure, will He bare
To the roots of thunder, if we kneel and sue?

III.

From Casa Guidi windows I looked forth,
And saw ten thousand eyes of Florentines
Flash back the triumph of the Lombard north,—
Saw fifty banners, freighted with the signs
And exultations of the awakened earth,
Float on above the multitude in lines,
Straight to the Pitti. So, the vision went.
And so, between those populous rough hands
Raised in the sun, Duke Leopold outleant,
And took the patriot's oath, which henceforth stands

Among the oaths of perjurers, eminent
To catch the lightnings ripened for these lands.

IV.

Why swear at all, thou false Duke Leopold?
What need to swear? What need to boast thy blood
Taintless of Austria, and thy heart unsold
Away from Florence? It was understood
God made thee not too vigorous or too bold,
And men had patience with thy quiet mood,
And women, pity, as they saw thee pace
Their festive streets with premature grey hairs:
We turned the mild dejection of thy face
To princely meanings, took thy wrinkling cares
For ruffling hopes, and called thee weak, not base.
Better to light the torches for more prayers

And smoke the pale Madonnas at the shrine,
Being still "our poor Grand-duke," "our good Grand-
duke,"
"Who cannot help the Austrian in his line,"
Than write an oath upon a nation's book
For men to spit at with scorn's blurring brine!
Who dares forgive what none can overlook?

V.

For me, I do repent me in this dust
Of towns and temples, which makes Italy,—
I sigh amid the sighs which breathe a gust
Of dying century to century,
Around us on the uneven crater-crust
Of the old worlds,—I bow my soul and knee,
And sigh and do repent me of my fault

That ever I believed the man was true.
  These sceptred strangers shun the common salt,
And, therefore, when the general board 's in view,
  They standing up to carve for blind and halt,
We should suspect the viands which ensue.
  And I repent that in this time and place,
Where all the corpse-lights of experience burn
  From Cæsar's and Lorenzo's festering race,
To illumine groping reasoners, I could learn
  No better counsel for a simple case
Than to put faith in princes, in my turn.
  Heavens! had the death-piles of the ancient years
Flared up in vain before me? Knew I not
  What stench arises from their purple gears,—
And how the sceptres witness whence they got
  Their briar-wood, crackling through the atmosphere's

Foul smoke, by princely perjuries, kept hot?

Forgive me, ghosts of patriots,—Brutus, thou,

Who trailest downhill into life again

Thy blood-weighed cloak, to indict me with thy slow

Reproachful eyes!—for being taught in vain

That while the illegitimate Cæsars show

Of meaner stature than the first full strain,

(Confessed incompetent to conquer Gaul)

They swoon as feebly and cross Rubicons

As rashly as any Julius of them all.

Forgive, that I forgot the mind that runs

Through absolute races, too unsceptical!

I saw the man among his little sons,

His lips warm with their kisses while he swore,—

And I, because I am a woman, I,

Who felt my own child's coming life before

The prescience of my soul, and held faith high,
I could not bear to think, whoever bore,
That lips, so warmed, could shape so cold a lie.

VI.

From Casa Guidi windows I looked out,
Again looked, and beheld a different sight.
The Duke had fled before the people's shout
"Long live the Duke!" A people, to speak right,
Should speak as soft as courtiers, lest a doubt
Turn gracious sovereign brows to curdled white.
Moreover that same dangerous shouting meant
Some gratitude for future favours, which
Were only promised;—the Constituent
Implied;—the whole being subject to the hitch
In motu proprios, very incident

To all these Czars, from Paul to Paulovitch.
  Whereat the people rose up in the dust
Of the Duke's flying feet, and shouted still,
  And loudly, only, this time, as was just,
Not "Live the Duke," who had fled, for good or ill
  But "Live the People," who remained and must,
The unrenounced and unrenounceable.

VII.

  Long live the people! How they lived! and boiled
And bubbled in the cauldron of the street!
  How the young blustered, nor the old recoiled,
And what a thunderous stir of tongues and feet
  Trod flat the palpitating bells, and foiled
The joy-guns of their echo, shattering it!
  How they pulled down the Duke's arms everywhere!

How they set up new café-signs, to show
  Where patriots might sip ices in pure air—
(Yet the fresh paint smelt somewhat). To and fro
  How marched the civic guard, and stopped to stare
When boys broke windows in a civic glow.
  How rebel songs were sung to loyal tunes,
And the pope cursed, in ecclesiastic metres!
  How all the Circoli grew large as moons,
And all the speakers, moonstruck!—thankful greeters
  Of prospects which struck poor the ducal boons,
A mere free press, and chambers!—frank repeaters
  Of great Guerazzi's praises. . . . "There 's a man
The father of the land!—who, truly great,
  Takes off that national disgrace and ban,
The farthing tax upon our Florence-gate,
  And saves Italia as he only can."

How all the nobles fled, and would not wait,
  Because they were most noble! which being so,
How the mob vowed to burn their palaces,
  Because they were too free to have leave to go.
How grown men raged at Austria's wickedness,
  And smoked,—while fifty striplings in a row
Marched straight to Piedmont for the wrong's redress!
  Who says we failed in duty, we who wore
Black velvet like Italian democrats,
  Who slashed our sleeves like patriots, nor forswore
The true republic in the form of hats?
  We chased the archbishop from the duomo door—
We chalked the walls with bloody caveats
  Against all tyrants. If we did not fight
Exactly, we fired muskets up the void,
  To show that victory was ours of right.

We met, discussed in every place, self-buoyed
  Except, perhaps, i' the chambers, day and night :
We proved that all the poor should be employed,
  And yet the rich not worked for anywise,—
Pay certified, yet payers abrogated,
  Full work secured, yet liabilities
To over-work excluded,—not one bated
  Of all our holidays, that still, at twice
Or thrice a-week, are moderately rated.
  We proved that Austria was dislodged, or would
Or should be, and that Tuscany in arms
  Should, would, dislodge her, in high hardihood !
And yet, to leave our piazzas, shops, and farms,
  For the bare sake of fighting, was not good.
We proved that also—" Did we carry charms
  Against being killed ourselves, that we should rush

On killing others? What! desert herewith
 Our wives and mothers!—was that duty? Tush!"
At which we shook the sword within the sheath,
 Like heroes—only louder! and the flush
Ran up our cheek to meet the victor's wreath.
 Nay, what we proved, we shouted—how we shouted,
(Especially the little boys did) planting
 That tree of liberty whose fruit is doubted
Because the roots are not of nature's granting—
 A tree of good and evil!—none, without it,
Grow gods!—alas, and, with it, men were wanting.

VIII.

 O holy knowledge, holy liberty,
O holy rights of nations! If I speak
 These bitter things against the jugglery

Of days that in your names proved blind and weak,
It is that tears are bitter. When we see
The brown skulls grin at death in churchyards bleak,
We do not cry, "This Yorick is too light,"—
For death grows deathlier with that mouth he makes.
So with my mocking. Bitter things I write,
Because my soul is bitter for your sakes,
O freedom! O my Florence!

IX.

Men who might
Do greatly in a universe that breaks
And burns, must ever *know* before they do.
Courage and patience are but sacrifice;
And sacrifice is offered for and to
Something conceived of. Each man pays a price

For what himself counts precious, whether true
Or false the appreciation it implies.
Here, was no knowledge, no conception, nought!
Desire was absent, that provides great deeds
From out the greatness of prevenient thought;
And action, action, like a flame that needs
A steady breath and fuel, being caught
Up, like a burning reed from other reeds,
Flashed in the empty and uncertain air,
Then wavered, then went out. Behold, who blames
A crooked course, when not a goal is there,
To round the fervid striving of the games?
An ignorance of means may minister
To greatness, but an ignorance of aims
Makes it impossible to be great at all.
So, with our Tuscans! Let none dare to say,

Here virtue never can be national,
Here fortitude can never cut its way
Between the Austrian muskets, out of thrall.
I tell you rather, that whoever may
Discern true ends here, shall grow pure enough
To love them, brave enough to strive for them,
And strong to reach them, though the roads be rough:
That having learnt—by no mere apophthegm—
Not the mere draping of a graceful stuff
About a statue, broidered at the hem,—
Not the mere trilling on an opera stage,
Of 'libertà' to bravos—(a fair word,
Yet too allied to inarticulate rage
And breathless sobs, for singing, though the chord
Were deeper than they struck it!)—but the gauge
Of civil wants sustained, and wrongs abhorred,—

The serious, sacred meaning and full use
Of freedom for a nation,—then, indeed,
Our Tuscans, underneath the bloody dews
Of a new morning, rising up agreed
And bold, will want no Saxon souls or thews,
To sweep their piazzas clear of Austria's breed.

X.

Alas, alas! it was not so this time.
Conviction was not, courage failed, and truth
Was something to be doubted of. The mime
Changed masks, because a mime; the tide as smooth
In running in as out; no sense of crime
Because no sense of virtue. Sudden ruth
Seized on the people . . . they would have again
Their good Grand-duke, and leave Guerazzi, though

He took that tax from Florence:—"Much in vain
He took it from the market-carts, we trow,
While urgent that no market-men remain,
But all march off, and leave the spade and plough,
To die among the Lombards. Was it thus
The dear paternal Duke did? Live the Duke!"
At which the joy bells multitudinous,
Swept by an opposite wind, as loudly shook.
Recall the mild Archbishop to his house,
To bless the people with his frightened look,
For he shall not be hanged yet, we intend.
Seize on Guerazzi; guard him in full view,
Or else we stab him in the back, to end.
Rub out those chalked devices! Set up new
The Duke's arms; doff your Phrygian caps; and mend
The pavement of the piazzas broke into

By the bare poles of freedom! Smooth the way
For the Duke's carriage, lest his highness sigh
"Here trees of liberty grew yesterday."
Long live the Duke!—How roared the cannonry,
How rocked each campanile, and through a spray
Of nosegays, wreaths, and kerchiefs, tossed on high,
How marched the civic guard, the people still
Shouting—especially the little boys!
Alas, poor people, of an unfledged will
Most fitly expressed by such a callow voice!
Alas, still poorer Duke, incapable
Of being worthy even of that noise!

XI.

You think he came back instantly, with thanks
And tears in his faint eyes, and hands extended

To stretch the franchise through their utmost ranks?
That having, like a father, apprehended,
He came to pardon fatherly those pranks
Played out, and now in filial service ended?—
That some love token, like a prince, he threw,
To meet the people's love-call, in return?
Well, how he came I will relate to you;
And if your hearts should burn, why, hearts *must* burn,
To make the ashes which things old and new
Shall be washed clean in—as this Duke will learn.

XII.

From Casa Guidi windows, gazing, then,
I saw and witness how the Duke came back.
The regular tramp of horse and tread of men
Did smite the silence like an anvil black

And sparkless. With her wide eyes at full strain,
Our Tuscan nurse exclaimed, "Alack, alack,
Signora! these shall be the Austrians." "Nay,
Hush, hush," I answered, "do not wake the child!"
For so, my two-months' baby sleeping lay
In milky dreams upon the bed and smiled;
And I thought "he shall sleep on, while he may,
Through the world's baseness. Not being yet defiled,
Why should he be disturbed by what is done?"
Then, gazing, I beheld the long-drawn street
Live out, from end to end, full in the sun,
With Austria's thousands. Sword and bayonet,
Horse, foot, artillery,—cannons rolling on,
Like blind, slow storm-clouds gestant with the heat
Of undeveloped lightnings, each bestrode
By a single man, dust-white from head to heel,

Indifferent as the dreadful thing he rode,
Calm as a sculptured Fate, and terrible!
As some smooth river which hath overflowed,
Doth slow and silent down its current wheel
A loosened forest, all the pines erect,—
So, swept, in mute significance of storm,
The marshalled thousands,—not an eye deflect
To left or right, to catch a novel form
Of the famed city adorned by architect
And carver, nor of Beauties live and warm
Scared at the casements,—all, straightforward eyes
And faces, held as steadfast as their swords,
And cognisant of acts, not imageries.
The key, O Tuscans, too well fits the wards!
Ye asked for mimes; these bring you tragedies—
For purple; these shall wear it as your lords.

Ye played like children: die like innocents!
Ye mimicked lightnings with a torch: the crack
Of the actual bolt, your pastime, circumvents.
Ye called up ghosts, believing they were slack
To follow any voice from Gilboa's tents, . . .
Here 's Samuel!—and, so, Grand-dukes come back!

XIII.

And yet, they are no prophets though they come.
That awful mantle they are drawing close,
Shall be searched, one day, by the shafts of Doom,
Through double folds now hoodwinking the brows.
Resuscitated monarchs disentomb
Grave-reptiles with them, in their new life-throes:
Let such beware. Behold, the people waits,
Like God. As He, in his serene of might,

So they, in their endurance of long straits.
Ye stamp no nation out, though day and night
Ye tread them with that absolute heel which grates
And grinds them flat from all attempted height.
You kill worms sooner with a garden-spade
Than you kill peoples: peoples will not die;
The tail curls stronger when you lop the head;
They writhe at every wound and multiply,
And shudder into a heap of life that 's made
Thus vital from God's own vitality.
'Tis hard to shrivel back a day of God's
Once fixed for judgment: 'tis as hard to change
The people's, when they rise beneath their loads
And heave them from their backs with violent wrench,
To crush the oppressor. For that judgment rod 's
The measure of this popular revenge.

XIV.

Meantime, from Casa Guidi windows we
Beheld the armament of Austria flow
Into the drowning heart of Tuscany.
And yet none wept, none cursed; or, if 'twas so,
They wept and cursed in silence. Silently
Our noisy Tuscans watched the invading foe;
They had learnt silence. Pressed against the wall
And grouped upon the church-steps opposite,
A few pale men and women stared at all.
God knows what they were feeling, with their white
Constrained faces!—they, so prodigal
Of cry and gesture when the world goes right,
Or wrong indeed. But here, was depth of wrong,
And here, still water: they were silent here:

And through that sentient silence, struck along
That measured tramp from which it stood out clear,
Distinct the sound and silence, like a gong
Tolled upon midnight,—each made awfuller;
While every soldier in his cap displayed
A leaf of olive. Dusty, bitter thing!
Was such plucked at Novara, is it said?

XV.

A cry is up in England, which doth ring
The hollow world through, that for ends of trade
And virtue, and God's better worshipping,
We henceforth should exalt the name of Peace,
And leave those rusty wars that eat the soul,—
(Besides their clippings at our golden fleece.)
I, too, have loved peace, and from bole to bole

Of immemorial, undeciduous trees,
Would write, as lovers use, upon a scroll
The holy name of Peace, and set it high
Where none should pluck it down. On trees, I
say,—
Not upon gibbets!—With the greenery
Of dewy branches and the flowery May,
Sweet mediation 'twixt the earth and sky,
Providing, for the shepherd's holiday!
Not upon gibbets!—though the vulture leaves
Some quiet to the bones he first picked bare.
Not upon dungeons! though the wretch who grieves
And groans within, stirs not the outer air
As much as little field-mice stir the sheaves.
Not upon chain-bolts! though the slave's despair
Has dulled his helpless, miserable brain,

And left him blank beneath the freeman's whip,
To sing and laugh out idiocies of pain.
Nor yet on starving homes! where many a lip
Has sobbed itself asleep through curses vain!
I love no peace which is not fellowship,
And which includes not mercy. I would have
Rather, the raking of the guns across
The world, and shrieks against Heaven's architrave.
Rather, the struggle in the slippery fosse,
Of dying men and horses, and the wave
Blood-bubbling. . . . Enough said!—By Christ's own cross,
And by the faint heart of my womanhood,
Such things are better than a Peace which sits
Beside the hearth in self-commended mood,
And takes no thought how wind and rain by fits

Are howling out of doors against the good
Of the poor wanderer. What! your peace admits
Of outside anguish while it sits at home?
I loathe to take its name upon my tongue—
It is no peace. 'Tis treason, stiff with doom,—
'Tis gagged despair, and inarticulate wrong,
Annihilated Poland, stifled Rome,
Dazed Naples, Hungary fainting 'neath the thong,
And Austria wearing a smooth olive-leaf
On her brute forehead, while her hoofs outpress
The life from these Italian souls, in brief.
O Lord of Peace, who art Lord of Righteousness,
Constrain the anguished worlds from sin and grief,
Pierce them with conscience, purge them with redress,
And give us peace which is no counterfeit!

XVI.

But wherefore should we look out any more
  From Casa Guidi windows? Shut them straight;
And let us sit down by the folded door
  And veil our saddened faces, and so, wait
What next the judgment-heavens make ready for.
  I have grown weary of these windows. Sights
Come thick enough and clear enough with thought,
  Without the sunshine; souls have inner lights:
And since the Grand-duke has come back and brought
  This army of the North which thus requites
His filial South, we leave him to be taught.
  His South, too, has learnt something certainly,
Whereof the practice will bring profit soon;
  And peradventure other eyes may see,

From Casa Guidi windows, what is done
  Or undone. Whatsoever deeds they be,
Pope Pius will be glorified in none.

XVII.

  Record that gain, Mazzini!—it shall top
Some heights of sorrow. Peter's rock, so named,
  Shall lure no vessel, any more, to drop
Among the breakers. Peter's chair is shamed
  Like any vulgar throne the nations lop
To pieces for their firewood unreclaimed;
  And, when it burns too, we shall see as well
In Italy as elsewhere. Let it burn.
  The cross, accounted still adorable,
Is Christ's cross only!—if the thief's would earn
  Some stealthy genuflexions, we rebel;

And here the impenitent thief's has had its turn,
As God knows; and the people on their knees
Scoff and toss back the croziers, stretched like yokes
To press their heads down lower by degrees.
So Italy, by means of these last strokes,
Escapes the danger which preceded these,
Of leaving captured hands in cloven oaks . . .
Of leaving very souls within the buckle
Whence bodies struggled outward . . . of supposing
That freemen may like bondsmen kneel and truckle,
And then stand up as usual, without losing
An inch of stature.
Those whom she-wolves suckle
Will bite as wolves do, in the grapple-closing
Of adverse interests: this, at last, is known,
(Thank Pius for the lesson) that albeit,

Among the Popedom's hundred heads of stone
Which blink down on you from the roof's retreat
In Siena's tiger-striped cathedral,—Joan
And Borgia 'mid their fellows you may greet,
A harlot and a devil, you will see
Not a man, still less angel, grandly set
With open soul, to render man more free.
The fishers are still thinking of the net,
And if not thinking of the hook too, we
Are counted somewhat deeply in their debt:
But that 's a rare case—so, by hook and crook
They take the advantage, agonizing Christ
By rustier nails than those of Cedron's brook,
I' the people's body very cheaply priced;
Quoting high priesthood out of Holy book,
And buying death-fields with the sacrificed.

XVIII.

Priests, priests!—there 's no such name,—God's own,
except
Ye take most vainly. Through Heaven's lifted gate
The priestly ephod in sole glory swept,
When Christ ascended, entered in, and sate
With victor face sublimely overwept,
At Deity's right hand, to mediate,
He alone, He for ever. On his breast
The Urim and the Thummim, fed with fire
From the full Godhead, flicker with the unrest
Of human, pitiful heartbeats. Come up higher,
All Christians! Levi's tribe is dispossest!
That solitary alb ye shall admire,
But not cast lots for. The last chrism, poured right,

Was on that Head, and poured for burial
  And not for domination in men's sight.
What are these churches? The old temple wall
  Doth overlook them juggling with the sleight
Of surplice, candlestick, and altar-pall.
  East church and west church, ay, north church and
      south,
Rome's church and England's,—let them all repent,
  And make concordats 'twixt their soul and mouth,
Succeed St. Paul by working at the tent,
  Become infallible guides by speaking truth,
And excommunicate their own pride that bent
  And cramped the souls of men.

                        Why, even here,
Priestcraft burns out; the twined linen blazes,
  Not, like asbestos, to grow white and clear,

But all to perish!—while the fire-smell raises
To life some swooning spirits who, last year,
Lost breath and heart in these church-stifled places.
Why, almost, through this Pius, we believed
The priesthood could be an honest thing, he smiled
So saintly while our corn was being sheaved
For his own granaries. Showing now defiled
His hireling hands, a better help 's achieved
Than if he blessed us shepherd-like and mild.
False doctrine, strangled by its own amen,
Dies in the throat of all this nation. Who
Will speak a pope's name, as they rise again?
What woman or what child will count him true?
What dreamer praise him with the voice or pen?
What man fight for him?—Pius has his due.

XIX.

Record that gain, Mazzini!—Yes, but first
Set down thy people's faults:—set down the want
Of soul-conviction; set down aims dispersed,
And incoherent means, and valour scant
Because of scanty faith, and schisms accursed
That wrench these brother-hearts from covenant
With freedom and each other. Set down this
And this, and see to overcome it when
The seasons bring the fruits thou wilt not miss
If wary. Let no cry of patriot men
Distract thee from the stern analysis
Of masses who cry only: keep thy ken
Clear as thy soul is virtuous. Heroes' blood
Splashed up against thy noble brow in Rome.—

Let such not blind thee to the interlude
Which was not also holy, yet did come
'Twixt sacramental actions:—brotherhood,
Despised even there,—and something of the doom
Of Remus, in the trenches. Listen now—
Rossi died silent near where Cæsar died.
HE did not say, "My Brutus, is it thou?"
Instead, rose Italy and testified,
"'Twas *I*, and *I* am Brutus.—I avow."
At which the whole world's laugh of scorn replied,
"A poor maimed copy of Brutus!"

Too much like,
Indeed, to be so unlike. Too unskilled
At Philippi and the honest battle-pike,
To be so skilful where a man is killed
Near Pompey's statue, and the daggers strike

At unawares i' the throat. Was thus fulfilled
An omen of great Michel Angelo,—
When Marcus Brutus he conceived complete,
And strove to hurl him out by blow on blow
Upon the marble, at Art's thunderheat,
Till haply some pre-shadow rising slow
Of what his Italy would fancy meet
To be called BRUTUS, straight his plastic hand
Fell back before his prophet soul, and left
A fragment . . . a maimed Brutus,—but more grand
Than this, so named of Rome, was!

Let thy weft
Be of one woof and warp, Mazzini!—stand
With no man of a spotless fame bereft—
Not for Italia! Neither stand apart,
No, not for the republic!—from those pure

Brave men who hold the level of thy heart
In patriot truth, as lover and as doer,
Albeit they will not follow where thou art
As extreme theorist. Trust and distrust fewer;
And so bind strong and keep unstained the cause
Which, at God's signal, war-trumps newly blown
Shall yet annuntiate to the world's applause.

XX.

Just now, the world is busy: it has grown
A Fair-going world. Imperial England draws
The flowing ends of the earth, from Fez, Canton,
Delhi and Stockholm, Athens and Madrid,
The Russias and the vast Americas,
As a queen gathers in her robes amid
Her golden cincture,—isles, peninsulas,

Capes, continents, far inland countries hid
By jaspar sands and hills of chrysopras,
All trailing in their splendours through the door
Of the new Crystal Palace. Every nation,
To every other nation, strange of yore,
Shall face to face give civic salutation,
And hold up in a proud right hand before
That congress, the best work which she could fashion
By her best means—"These corals, will you please
To match against your oaks? They grow as fast
Within my wilderness of purple seas."—
"This diamond stared upon me as I passed
(As a live god's eye from a marble frieze)
Along a dark of diamonds. Is it classed?"—
"I wove these stuffs so subtly, that the gold
Swims to the surface of the silk, like cream,

And curdles to fair patterns. Ye behold!"—
"These delicated muslins rather seem
Than be, you think? Nay, touch them and be bold,
Though such veiled Chakhi's face in Hafiz' dream."—
"These carpets—you walk slow on them like kings,
Inaudible like spirits, while your foot
Dips deep in velvet roses and such things."—
"Even Apollonius might commend this flute.*
The music, winding through the stops, upsprings
To make the player very rich. Compute."—
"Here's goblet-glass, to take in with your wine
The very sun its grapes were ripened under.
Drink light and juice together, and each fine."—

* Philostratus relates of Apollonius that he objected to the musical instrument of Linus the Rhodian, its incompetence to enrich and beautify. The history of music in our day, would, upon the former point, sufficiently confute the philosopher.

"This model of a steam-ship moves your wonder?
You should behold it crushing down the brine,
Like a blind Jove who feels his way with thunder."—
"Here's sculpture! Ah, *we* live too! Why not throw
Our life into our marbles? Art has place
For other artists after Angelo."—
"I tried to paint out here a natural face—
For nature includes Raffael, as we know,
Not Raffael nature. Will it help my case?"—
"Methinks you will not match this steel of ours!"—
"Nor you this porcelain! One might think the clay
Retained in it the larvæ of the flowers,
They bud so, round the cup, the old spring way."—
"Nor you these carven woods, where birds in bowers,
With twisting snakes and climbing cupids, play."

XXI.

O Magi of the east and of the west,
Your incense, gold, and myrrh are excellent.—
What gifts for Christ, then, bring ye with the rest?
Your hands have worked well. Is your courage spent
In handwork only? Have you nothing best,
Which generous souls may perfect and present,
And He shall thank the givers for? No light
Of teaching, liberal nations, for the poor,
Who sit in darkness when it is not night?
No cure for wicked children? Christ,—no cure!
No help for women sobbing out of sight
Because men made the laws? No brothel-lure
Burnt out by popular lightnings?—Hast thou found

No remedy, my England, for such woes?
  No outlet, Austria, for the scourged and bound,
No entrance for the exiled? No repose,
  Russia, for knouted Poles worked underground,
And gentle ladies bleached among the snows?—
  No mercy for the slave, America?—
No hope for Rome, free France, chivalric France?—
  Alas, great nations have great shames, I say.
No pity, O world, no tender utterance
  Of benediction, and prayers stretched this way
To poor Italia baffled by mischance?—
  O gracious nations, give some ear to me!
You all go to your Fair, and I am one
  Who at the roadside of humanity
Beseech your alms,—a justice to be done.
  So, prosper!

XXII.

In the name of Italy,
Meantime, her patriot dead have benizon!
They only have done well; and what they did
Being perfect, it shall triumph. Let them slumber.
No king of Egypt in a pyramid
Is safer from oblivion, though he number
Full seventy cerements for a coverlid.
These Dead be seeds of life, and shall encumber
The sad heart of the land until it loose
The clammy clods and let out the spring-growth
In beatific green through every bruise.
The tyrant should take heed to what he doth,
Since every victim-carrion turns to use,
And drives a chariot, like a god made wroth,

Against each piled injustice. Ay, the least
Dead for Italia, not in vain has died,
However vainly, ere life's struggle ceased,
To mad dissimilar ends they swerved aside.
Each grave her nationality has pieced
By its own noble breadth, and fortified,
And pinned it deeper to the soil. Forlorn
Of thanks, be, therefore, no one of these graves!
Not Hers,—who, at her husband's side, in scorn,
Outfaced the whistling shot and hissing waves,
Until she felt her little babe unborn
Recoil, within her, from the violent staves
And bloodhounds of the world: at which, her life
Dropt inwards from her eyes, and followed it
Beyond the hunters. Garibaldi's wife
And child died so. And now, the sea-weeds fit

Her body like a proper shroud and coif,
And murmurously the ebbing waters grit
The little pebbles, while she lies interred
In the sea-sand. Perhaps, ere dying thus,
She looked up in his face which never stirred
From its clenched anguish, as to make excuse
For leaving him for his, if so she erred.
Well he remembers that she could not choose.
A memorable grave! Another is
At Genoa, where a king may fitly lie,—
Who bursting that heroic heart of his
At lost Novara, that he could not die,
Though thrice into the cannon's eyes for this
He plunged his shuddering steed, and felt the sky
Reel back between the fire-shocks;—stripped away
The ancestral ermine ere the smoke had cleared,

And naked to the soul, that none might say
His kingship covered what was base and bleared
With treason, he went out an exile, yea,
An exiled patriot! Let him be revered.

XXIII.

Yea, verily, Charles Albert has died well:
And if he lived not all so, as one spoke,
The sin pass softly with the passing bell.
For he was shriven, I think, in cannon smoke,
And taking off his crown, made visible
A hero's forehead. Shaking Austria's yoke
He shattered his own hand and heart. 'So best,'
His last words were upon his lonely bed,—
'I do not end like popes and dukes at least—
'Thank God for it.' And now that he is dead,

Admitting it is proved and manifest
That he was worthy, with a discrowned head,
To measure heights with patriots, let them stand
Beside the man in his Oporto shroud,
And each vouchsafe to take him by the hand,
And kiss him on the cheek, and say aloud,
'Thou, too, hast suffered for our native land!
'My brother, thou art one of us. Be proud.'

XXIV.

Still, graves, when Italy is talked upon!
Still, still, the patriot's tomb, the stranger's hate.
Still Niobe! still fainting in the sun
By whose most dazzling arrows violate
Her beauteous offspring perished! Has she won
Nothing but garlands for the graves, from Fate?

Nothing but death-songs?—Yet, be it understood,
Life throbs in noble Piedmont! while the feet
Of Rome's clay image, dabbled soft in blood,
Grow flat with dissolution, and, as meet,
Will soon be shovelled off, like other mud,
To leave the passage free in church and street.
And I, who first took hope up in this song,
Because a child was singing one . . . behold,
The hope and omen were not, haply, wrong!
Poets are soothsayers still, like those of old
Who studied flights of doves,—and creatures young
And tender, mighty meanings, may unfold.

XXV.

The sun strikes, through the windows, up the floor:
Stand out in it, my own young Florentine,

Not two years old, and let me see thee more!
It grows along thy amber curls, to shine
Brighter than elsewhere. Now, look straight before,
And fix thy brave blue English eyes on mine,
And from thy soul, which fronts the future so,
With unabashed and unabated gaze,
Teach me to hope for, what the Angels know,
When they smile clear as thou dost. Down God's ways,
With just alighted feet between the snow
And snowdrops, where a little lamb may graze,
Thou hast no fear, my lamb, about the road,
Albeit in our vain-glory we assume
That, less than we have, thou hast learnt of God.
Stand out, my blue-eyed prophet!—thou, to whom
The earliest world-day light that ever flowed,
Through Casa Guidi windows, chanced to come!

Now shake the glittering nimbus of thy hair,
And be God's witness;—that the elemental
New springs of life are gushing everywhere,
To cleanse the water courses, and prevent all
Concrete obstructions which infest the air!
—That earth 's alive, and gentle or ungentle
Motions within her, signify but growth:
The ground swells greenest o'er the labouring moles.
Howe'er the uneasy world is vexed and wroth,
Young children, lifted high on parent souls,
Look round them with a smile upon the mouth,
And take for music every bell that tolls.

Who said we should be better if like these?
And *we* . . . despond we for the future, though
Posterity is smiling at our knees,
Convicting us of folly? Let us go—

We will trust God. The blank interstices
Men take for ruins, He will build into
With pillared marbles rare, or knit across
With generous arches, till the fane 's complete.
This world has no perdition, if some loss.

XXVI.

Such cheer I gather from thy smiling, Sweet!
The self same cherub faces which emboss
The rail, lean inward to the mercy-seat.

NOTES.

Page 4, l. 5.

"Void at Verona," &c.

They show at Verona an empty trough of stone as the tomb of Juliet.

Page 6, l. 13.

"That's Michel Angelo! his statues wait."

In the Sagrestia Nuova, where the statues of Day and Night, Dawn and Twilight, recline on the tombs of Giuliano de' Medici, third son of Lorenzo the Magnificent, and Lorenzo of Urbino, his grandson. Strozzi's epigram on the Night, with Michel Angelo's rejoinder, is well known.

Page 8, l. 3.

"Thou wert commanded to build up in snow."

This mocking task was set by Pietro, the unworthy successor of Lorenzo the Magnificent.

Page 18, l. 9.

" When men make record, with the flowers they strew,
'Savonarola's soul,'" &c.

Savonarola was burnt in martyrdom for his testimony against Papal corruptions as early as March, 1498: and, as late as our own day, it is a custom in Florence to strew violets on the pavement where he suffered, in grateful recognition of the anniversary.

Page 23, l. 3.

" ——where, at plague-time, Macchiavel.'

See his description of the plague in Florence.

Page 24, l. 1.

"A king stood bare before its sovran grace."

Charles of Anjou, whom, in his passage through Florence, Cimabue allowed to see this picture while yet in his "Bottega." The populace followed the royal visitor, and in the universal delight and admiration, the quarter of the city in which the artist lived was called "Borgo Allegri." The picture was carried in a triumph to the church and deposited there.

Page 25, l. 13.

" Yet rightly was young Giotto talked about,
Whom Cimabue found among the sheep."

How Cimabue found Giotto, the shepherd-boy, sketching a ram

of his flock upon a stone, is a pretty story told by Vasari,—who also relates how the elder artist Margheritone died "infastidito" of the successes of the new school.

Page 43, l. 5.

"——*in Santa Croce church, forlorn*
Of any corpse,' &c.

The Florentines, to whom the Ravennese denied the body of Dante which was asked of them in a "late remorse of love," have given a cenotaph to their divine poet in this church. Something less than a grave!

Page 43, l. 13.

"*Good lovers of our age to track and plough.*"

In allusion to Mr. Kirkup's well-known discovery of Giotto's fresco-portrait of Dante.

Page 80, l. 14.

"*From Tuscan Bellosguardo*," &c

Galileo's villa near Florence is built on an eminence called Bellosguardo.

LONDON
BRADBURY AND EVANS, PRINTERS, WHITEFRIARS

www.ingramcontent.com/pod-product-compliance
Ingram Content Group UK Ltd.
Pitfield, Milton Keynes, MK11 3LW, UK
UKHW042152280225
455719UK00001B/280